CONTENTS

1. INTRODUCTION
2. SETTING FINANCIAL GOALS
3. UNDERSTANDING RISK AND RETURN
4. CREATING A BUDGET AND SAVING FOR INVESTMENT
5. EXPLORING INVESTMENT OPTIONS
6. STOCKS: THE BASICS
7. BONDS: A STEADY INCOME STREAM
8. MUTUAL FUNDS AND EXCHANGE-TRADED FUNDS (ETFS)
9. DIVERSIFICATION: THE KEY TO RISK MANAGEMENT
10. LONG-TERM INVESTING AND THE POWER OF COMPOUND INTEREST
11. INVESTING IN REAL ESTATE
12. BUILDING A PORTFOLIO: ASSET ALLOCATION STRATEGIES
13. THE IMPORTANCE OF RESEARCH AND DUE DILIGENCE
14. TAX CONSIDERATIONS AND RETIREMENT ACCOUNTS
15. DEVELOPING AN INVESTMENT PLAN
16. STAYING INFORMED AND ADAPTING TO MARKET CHANGES
17. COMMON PITFALLS AND HOW TO AVOID THEM
18. CONCLUSION: YOUR JOURNEY BEGINS HERE

INTRODUCTION

WELCOME TO THE WORLD OF INVESTING! IN THIS FIRST CHAPTER, WE WILL LAY THE FOUNDATION FOR YOUR JOURNEY INTO THE EXCITING AND POTENTIALLY REWARDING REALM OF INVESTMENT. WE WILL EXPLORE WHAT INVESTING IS, WHY IT MATTERS, AND THE OPPORTUNITIES IT PRESENTS FOR ACHIEVING YOUR FINANCIAL GOALS. WHETHER YOU'RE A NOVICE OR HAVE SOME BASIC KNOWLEDGE, THIS CHAPTER WILL SET THE STAGE FOR YOUR INVESTMENT EDUCATION.

IN THE FOLLOWING CHAPTERS, WE WILL DELVE DEEPER INTO VARIOUS INVESTMENT OPTIONS, RISK MANAGEMENT STRATEGIES, AND TECHNIQUES FOR BUILDING A DIVERSIFIED PORTFOLIO. SO, GET READY TO EXPAND YOUR FINANCIAL HORIZONS AND DISCOVER THE POTENTIAL REWARDS THAT AWAIT YOU IN THE WORLD OF INVESTING.

Setting Financial Goals

BEFORE EMBARKING ON YOUR INVESTMENT JOURNEY, IT IS ESSENTIAL TO ESTABLISH CLEAR AND REALISTIC FINANCIAL GOALS. SETTING GOALS PROVIDES YOU WITH A ROADMAP, MOTIVATION, AND A SENSE OF PURPOSE FOR YOUR INVESTMENTS. IN THIS CHAPTER, WE WILL DELVE INTO THE PROCESS OF SETTING FINANCIAL GOALS AND HOW THEY SHAPE YOUR INVESTMENT STRATEGY.

1. Reflect on Your Aspirations: Begin by reflecting on your long-term aspirations and what you hope to achieve through investing. Consider questions such as:
   - What are your dreams and aspirations for the future?
   - Do you want to retire comfortably?
   - Do you have any specific financial milestones, such as buying a house or starting a business?
   - Are you planning for your children's education?

2. Define Specific and Measurable Goals: To make your goals actionable, it is crucial to define them specifically and make them measurable. For example:
   - Instead of saying, "I want to retire comfortably," define the desired retirement age and the amount of money you would like to have saved by then.
   - If you plan to buy a house, determine the target purchase price, down payment amount, and the desired timeframe.

3. Prioritize Your Goals:
Consider the importance and urgency of your various financial goals. Some goals may have a higher priority than others, depending on your circumstances and personal values. Assigning priorities will help you allocate your resources effectively.

4. Set Realistic Timeframes: Determine realistic timeframes for achieving each goal. Short-term goals may range from a few months to a few years, while long-term goals could span several decades. Be mindful of your time horizon, as it will influence your investment strategy.

5. Assess Your Risk Tolerance: Consider your risk tolerance, which refers to your comfort level with the potential ups and downs of investment returns. Assess your willingness and ability to withstand fluctuations in the value of your investments. This assessment will help you align your investment choices with your risk tolerance.

6. Quantify Your Goals: Assign a financial value to each goal. For example:
- Calculate the amount of money needed for retirement based on your desired lifestyle and estimated expenses.
- Determine the cost of your child's education, factoring in inflation and expected duration of study.

7. Break Goals into Milestones: Divide long-term goals into shorter-term milestones to track your progress and maintain motivation. These milestones will serve as checkpoints along your investment journey.

8. Review and Revise: Periodically review your goals to ensure they remain relevant and aligned with your evolving circumstances. Adjustments may be necessary due to changes in income, expenses, or personal circumstances.

CONCLUSION: SETTING CLEAR AND WELL-DEFINED FINANCIAL GOALS IS A CRUCIAL STEP IN YOUR INVESTMENT JOURNEY. IT PROVIDES DIRECTION, MOTIVATION, AND A FRAMEWORK FOR MAKING INVESTMENT DECISIONS. TAKE THE TIME TO REFLECT ON YOUR ASPIRATIONS, DEFINE YOUR GOALS, AND PRIORITIZE THEM ACCORDING TO YOUR VALUES. BY SETTING REALISTIC TIMEFRAMES, ASSESSING RISK TOLERANCE, AND QUANTIFYING YOUR GOALS, YOU WILL BE BETTER EQUIPPED TO DEVELOP AN EFFECTIVE INVESTMENT STRATEGY THAT CAN HELP YOU ACHIEVE FINANCIAL SUCCESS.

Understanding Risk and Return

INVESTING INVOLVES AN INHERENT TRADE-OFF BETWEEN RISK AND RETURN. IN THIS CHAPTER, WE WILL EXPLORE THE CONCEPT OF RISK AND RETURN AND UNDERSTAND HOW THEY ARE INTERCONNECTED. BY GAINING A COMPREHENSIVE UNDERSTANDING OF RISK AND RETURN, YOU WILL BE BETTER EQUIPPED TO MAKE INFORMED INVESTMENT DECISIONS.

1. What is Risk?
   - Definition of risk in the context of investments.
   - Different types of risks: market risk, inflation risk, interest rate risk, credit risk, and liquidity risk.
   - Understanding the concept of volatility and its relationship to risk.

2. Assessing Risk Tolerance:
   - Determining your risk tolerance by considering factors such as age, financial goals, investment time horizon, and personal comfort level.
   - Evaluating your ability to take risks based on factors like income stability, savings, and financial obligations.

3. Return on Investments:
   - Definition of return and its various forms: capital gains, dividends, interest, and rental income.
   - Calculation of investment returns: simple returns, compound returns, and annualized returns.
   - Historical performance analysis as a tool for evaluating potential returns.

4. Risk-Return Trade-Off:
   - Understanding the relationship between risk and return: higher returns typically come with higher risks, and lower risks are associated with lower returns.
   - Examples of low-risk and low-return investments, high-risk and high-return investments, and balanced options in between.

5. Diversification:
   - The importance of diversification in managing investment risk.
   - Exploring asset allocation strategies to balance risk and return across different investment classes.
   - Understanding correlation and its role in diversification.

6. Risk Management Techniques:
   - Setting stop-loss orders and employing risk management tools to limit potential losses.
   - The significance of regular portfolio monitoring and rebalancing.
   - Utilizing hedging strategies and protective options to manage risk.

7. Evaluating Investment Risks:
   - Conducting thorough research and due diligence before making investment decisions.
   - Analyzing company fundamentals, financial statements, and economic indicators.
   - Assessing the risk factors specific to different investment options.

8. **Risk vs. Reward Ratio:**
   - Examining risk-adjusted returns and understanding metrics such as the Sharpe ratio and the Sortino ratio.
   - Identifying investments that offer favorable risk-reward profiles.

9. **Long-Term Investing:**
   - Recognizing the impact of time horizon on risk and return.
   - Understanding the benefits of a long-term investment approach in mitigating short-term volatility.

10. **Behavioural Biases and Risk:**
    - Common behavioural biases that affect investment decision-making, such as loss aversion and herd mentality.
    - Strategies to mitigate biases and make rational investment choices.

CONCLUSION: UNDERSTANDING THE RELATIONSHIP BETWEEN RISK AND RETURN IS ESSENTIAL FOR SUCCESSFUL INVESTING. BY ASSESSING YOUR RISK TOLERANCE, DIVERSIFYING YOUR PORTFOLIO, AND PRACTICING SOUND RISK MANAGEMENT TECHNIQUES, YOU CAN STRIKE A BALANCE BETWEEN RISK AND RETURN THAT ALIGNS WITH YOUR INVESTMENT GOALS. REMEMBER THAT RISK IS INHERENT IN INVESTING, BUT WITH CAREFUL CONSIDERATION AND A LONG-TERM PERSPECTIVE, YOU CAN NAVIGATE THE INVESTMENT LANDSCAPE AND STRIVE FOR OPTIMAL RETURNS WHILE MANAGING RISK EFFECTIVELY.

Creating a Budget and Saving for Investment

BEFORE YOU CAN START INVESTING, IT IS IMPORTANT TO ESTABLISH A SOLID FINANCIAL FOUNDATION. IN THIS CHAPTER, WE WILL GUIDE YOU THROUGH THE PROCESS OF CREATING A BUDGET AND DEVELOPING EFFECTIVE SAVING HABITS TO ACCUMULATE THE NECESSARY FUNDS FOR INVESTMENT.

1. Assessing Your Current Financial Situation:
- Evaluating your income, expenses, and overall financial health.
- Tracking your spending patterns and identifying areas where you can cut back or save.

2. Setting Financial Goals:
- Reviewing the financial goals discussed in Chapter 2 and understanding how they influence your budgeting and saving strategies.
- Breaking down your goals into manageable milestones.

3. Creating a Budget:
- Developing a comprehensive budget that reflects your income, expenses, and financial goals.
- Categorizing your expenses into essential (e.g., housing, utilities, groceries) and discretionary (e.g., entertainment, dining out) categories.
- Allocating a portion of your income towards savings and investments.

4. **Identifying Areas for Cost Reduction:**
   - Analyzing your expenses and identifying areas where you can reduce costs.
   - Implementing strategies such as negotiating bills, cutting unnecessary subscriptions, and finding more affordable alternatives.

5. **Automating Savings:**
   - Setting up automatic transfers from your income to a separate savings or investment account.
   - Utilizing technology and apps to help track your progress and automate savings contributions.

6. **Emergency Fund:**
   - Understanding the importance of building an emergency fund to cover unexpected expenses.
   - Determining an appropriate amount for your emergency fund based on your financial circumstances and comfort level.

7. **Paying Off High-Interest Debt:**
   - Prioritizing the repayment of high-interest debt, such as credit cards or personal loans.
   - Adopting debt repayment strategies like the snowball method or the avalanche method.

8. **Maximizing Income:**
   - Exploring opportunities to increase your income, such as seeking career advancements, taking on additional work, or exploring side hustles.
   - Allocating any additional income towards your savings and investment goals.

9. Saving for Short-Term and Long-Term Goals:
- Allocating a portion of your savings towards short-term goals, such as a down payment for a house or a vacation.
- Allocating a portion towards long-term investment goals, such as retirement or education funds.

10. Reviewing and Adjusting Your Budget:
- Regularly reviewing your budget to ensure it aligns with your current financial situation and goals.
- Making adjustments as needed to accommodate changes in income, expenses, or priorities.

11. Staying Disciplined and Motivated:
- Developing discipline and consistency in following your budget and saving plan.
- Celebrating milestones and progress towards your financial goals to stay motivated.

CONCLUSION: CREATING A BUDGET AND DEVELOPING EFFECTIVE SAVING HABITS ARE CRUCIAL STEPS IN PREPARING FOR INVESTMENT. BY ASSESSING YOUR FINANCIAL SITUATION, SETTING GOALS, AND CREATING A BUDGET THAT PRIORITIZES SAVINGS, YOU CAN ACCUMULATE THE NECESSARY FUNDS TO EMBARK ON YOUR INVESTMENT JOURNEY. REMEMBER TO REVIEW AND ADJUST YOUR BUDGET REGULARLY, STAY DISCIPLINED, AND KEEP YOUR LONG-TERM FINANCIAL GOALS IN MIND. WITH CAREFUL PLANNING AND COMMITMENT, YOU WILL BE WELL ON YOUR WAY TO ACHIEVING FINANCIAL SUCCESS THROUGH INVESTMENTS.

EXPLORING INVESTMENT OPTIONS

AS A BEGINNER INVESTOR, IT IS IMPORTANT TO UNDERSTAND THE VARIOUS INVESTMENT OPTIONS AVAILABLE TO YOU. IN THIS CHAPTER, WE WILL EXPLORE SOME COMMON INVESTMENT OPTIONS AND PROVIDE AN OVERVIEW OF THEIR CHARACTERISTICS, BENEFITS, AND CONSIDERATIONS.

1. Stocks:
   - Explaining the basics of stocks, which represent ownership in a company.
   - Understanding how stocks are bought and sold through stock exchanges.
   - Discussing the potential risks and rewards associated with investing in stocks.

2. Bonds:
   - Defining bonds as debt securities issued by governments, municipalities, and corporations.
   - Exploring different types of bonds, such as government bonds, corporate bonds, and municipal bonds.
   - Highlighting the income-generating potential and relative stability of bond investments.

3. Mutual Funds:
   - Introducing mutual funds as investment vehicles that pool money from multiple investors to invest in a diversified portfolio of stocks, bonds, or other assets.
   - Discussing the benefits of diversification, professional management, and accessibility offered by mutual funds.
   - Examining different types of mutual funds, including equity funds, bond funds, and index funds.

4. Exchange-Traded Funds (ETFs):
   - Explaining ETFs as investment funds that trade on stock exchanges, similar to individual stocks.
   - Highlighting the benefits of diversification, liquidity, and lower expenses associated with ETFs.
   - Discussing different types of ETFs, such as equity ETFs, bond ETFs, and sector-specific ETFs.

5. Real Estate:
   - Introducing real estate as an investment option, including rental properties, real estate investment trusts (REITs), and real estate crowdfunding.
   - Discussing the potential benefits of real estate investments, such as income generation, tax advantages, and potential appreciation.
   - Highlighting the considerations and risks associated with real estate investing.

6. Commodities:
   - Explaining commodities as raw materials or primary goods that can be bought and sold, such as gold, oil, or agricultural products.
   - Discussing the factors that impact commodity prices and the risks involved in commodity investing.
   - Highlighting different ways to invest in commodities, such as through commodity futures contracts or exchange-traded funds.

7. **Options and Futures:**
   - Introducing options and futures as derivative instruments that derive their value from an underlying asset, such as stocks or commodities.
   - Exploring the speculative and hedging opportunities provided by options and futures contracts.
   - Highlighting the complexities and risks associated with options and futures trading.

8. **Cryptocurrencies:**
   - Discussing the emergence of cryptocurrencies, such as Bitcoin and Ethereum, as a new investment asset class.
   - Exploring the potential benefits and risks associated with investing in cryptocurrencies.
   - Highlighting the need for thorough research and understanding of the crypto market before investing.

9. **Other Investment Options:**
   - Briefly mentioning alternative investments like hedge funds, private equity, and venture capital.
   - Discussing the unique characteristics, risks, and potential rewards of these investment options.

<u>CONCLUSION</u>: UNDERSTANDING THE VARIOUS INVESTMENT OPTIONS AVAILABLE TO YOU IS CRUCIAL FOR BUILDING A DIVERSIFIED INVESTMENT PORTFOLIO. BY EXPLORING STOCKS, BONDS, MUTUAL FUNDS, ETFS, REAL ESTATE, COMMODITIES, OPTIONS AND FUTURES, CRYPTOCURRENCIES, AND OTHER INVESTMENT OPTIONS, YOU CAN MAKE INFORMED DECISIONS THAT ALIGN WITH YOUR FINANCIAL GOALS, RISK TOLERANCE, AND TIME HORIZON. REMEMBER TO CONDUCT THOROUGH RESEARCH, CONSIDER PROFESSIONAL ADVICE IF NECESSARY, AND CHOOSE INVESTMENTS THAT SUIT YOUR INDIVIDUAL CIRCUMSTANCES AND OBJECTIVES.

Stocks: The Basics

STOCKS REPRESENT OWNERSHIP IN A COMPANY AND OFFER INVESTORS THE OPPORTUNITY TO PARTICIPATE IN ITS GROWTH AND SUCCESS. IN THIS CHAPTER, WE WILL COVER THE FUNDAMENTALS OF STOCKS, INCLUDING HOW THEY WORK, THE DIFFERENT TYPES OF STOCKS, AND KEY CONSIDERATIONS FOR INVESTING IN THEM.

1. What are Stocks?
   - Definition of stocks as shares of ownership in a company.
   - Explanation of the stock market and stock exchanges where stocks are bought and sold.

2. How Stocks Work:
   - Overview of how companies issue stocks to raise capital.
   - Explanation of the primary and secondary markets for buying and selling stocks.
   - Introduction to stock indices as benchmarks for tracking stock market performance.

3. Common Stock vs. Preferred Stock:
   - Differentiating between common stock and preferred stock.
   - Explaining the voting rights and potential dividend preferences associated with each type.

4. **Benefits of Investing in Stocks:**
   - Potential for capital appreciation as the value of stocks increases over time.
   - Possibility of receiving dividends as a share of the company's profits.
   - Ability to participate in a company's growth and success.

5. **Risks Associated with Stocks:**
   - Volatility and fluctuations in stock prices.
   - Company-specific risks, such as poor financial performance or management issues.
   - Market risks, including economic downturns and changes in investor sentiment.

6. **Factors Affecting Stock Prices:**
   - Supply and demand dynamics in the stock market.
   - Company-specific factors, such as earnings reports, product launches, or legal issues.
   - Macroeconomic factors, such as interest rates, inflation, or geopolitical events.

7. **Fundamental Analysis:**
   - Overview of fundamental analysis, which involves evaluating a company's financial health, competitive position, and growth prospects.
   - Key financial metrics to consider, including earnings per share (EPS), price-to-earnings (P/E) ratio, and return on equity (ROE).

8. **Technical Analysis:**
   - Introduction to technical analysis, which involves studying stock price patterns and trends to predict future price movements.
   - Common technical analysis tools, such as moving averages, support and resistance levels, and chart patterns.

9. **Building a Diversified Stock Portfolio:**
- Importance of diversification to mitigate risk.
- Spreading investments across different sectors, industries, and market caps.
- Considering a mix of growth stocks, value stocks, and income stocks.

10. **Investment Strategies:**
- Long-term investing: Holding stocks for an extended period to benefit from compounding returns and ride out short-term market fluctuations.
- Value investing: Seeking undervalued stocks based on fundamental analysis and long-term growth potential.
- Growth investing: Identifying companies with strong growth prospects and investing in their stocks, even if they have higher valuations.

11. **Risks and Mitigation Strategies:**
- Setting realistic expectations and understanding that investing in stocks involves inherent risks.
- Implementing risk management techniques, such as diversification, regular portfolio reviews, and setting stop-loss orders.

CONCLUSION: STOCKS ARE AN ESSENTIAL COMPONENT OF MANY INVESTMENT PORTFOLIOS, OFFERING THE POTENTIAL FOR LONG-TERM CAPITAL APPRECIATION, DIVIDEND INCOME, AND PARTICIPATION IN A COMPANY'S SUCCESS. BY UNDERSTANDING THE BASICS OF STOCKS, THE TYPES AVAILABLE, THE FACTORS AFFECTING THEIR PRICES, AND THE IMPORTANCE OF DIVERSIFICATION, YOU CAN MAKE INFORMED INVESTMENT DECISIONS. REMEMBER TO CONDUCT THOROUGH RESEARCH, ANALYZE COMPANIES' FINANCIAL HEALTH, AND CONSIDER YOUR RISK TOLERANCE AND INVESTMENT GOALS WHEN INVESTING IN STOCKS.

Bonds: A Steady Income Stream

BONDS ARE FIXED-INCOME SECURITIES THAT OFFER INVESTORS A STEADY INCOME STREAM AND RELATIVE STABILITY COMPARED TO OTHER INVESTMENT OPTIONS. IN THIS CHAPTER, WE WILL EXPLORE THE BASICS OF BONDS, THEIR CHARACTERISTICS, TYPES, AND CONSIDERATIONS FOR INVESTING IN THEM.

1. What are Bonds?
   - Definition of bonds as debt instruments issued by governments, municipalities, and corporations to raise capital.
   - Explanation of how bonds work, including the coupon rate, maturity date, and principal value.

2. Characteristics of Bonds:
   - Fixed Income: Bonds provide regular interest payments, known as coupon payments, to bondholders.
   - Maturity Date: Bonds have a specified maturity date when the principal amount is repaid to the bondholder.
   - Credit Quality: Bonds have credit ratings that indicate the issuer's creditworthiness and risk of default.
   - Yield: Bonds have a yield that represents the return an investor receives based on the bond's price and coupon payments.

3. Types of Bonds:
   - Government Bonds: Bonds issued by national governments, such as Treasury bonds in the United States.
   - Municipal Bonds: Bonds issued by local governments or municipalities to fund public projects.

- Corporate Bonds: Bonds issued by corporations to raise capital for various purposes.
- Treasury Inflation-Protected Securities (TIPS): Bonds designed to protect against inflation by adjusting the principal value based on changes in the Consumer Price Index (CPI).

4. Benefits of Investing in Bonds:
- Regular Income Stream: Bonds provide predictable coupon payments, making them suitable for income-oriented investors.
- Relative Stability: Bonds generally offer more stability compared to stocks, with lower volatility and lower risk of capital loss.
- Diversification: Including bonds in a portfolio can help balance risk and potentially reduce overall portfolio volatility.

5. Risks Associated with Bonds:
- Interest Rate Risk: Bond prices are inversely related to interest rates, so rising rates can lead to price declines.
- Credit Risk: There is a risk that the issuer may default on interest payments or fail to repay the principal amount.
- Inflation Risk: Inflation erodes the purchasing power of fixed coupon payments over time.

6. Bond Ratings and Credit Analysis:
- Understanding bond ratings provided by credit rating agencies, such as Moody's, Standard & Poor's, and Fitch.
- Exploring factors considered in credit analysis, including the issuer's financial health, repayment ability, and economic conditions.

7. **Yield and Yield Curve:**
   - Explaining bond yield as the annual return on investment based on the bond's current price and coupon payments.
   - Understanding the yield curve, which plots yields of bonds with different maturities, and its implications for the economy and interest rate expectations.

8. **Bond Duration and Convexity:**
   - Explaining bond duration as a measure of its sensitivity to changes in interest rates.
   - Understanding convexity as a measure of the bond's price sensitivity to changes in interest rates.

9. **Building a Bond Portfolio:**
   - Determining investment objectives and risk tolerance to select appropriate bonds.
   - Balancing bond types, maturities, and credit quality to achieve diversification.
   - Considering laddering or barbelling strategies to manage interest rate risk.

10. **Bond Mutual Funds and ETFs:**
    - Introduction to bond mutual funds and exchange-traded funds (ETFs) as investment vehicles that provide diversified exposure to bonds.
    - Understanding the benefits and considerations of investing in bond funds compared to individual bonds.

11. **Risks and Mitigation Strategies:**
    - Assessing and managing interest rate risk by diversifying maturities or utilizing bond duration strategies.

- Evaluating credit risk by conducting thorough credit analysis and diversifying across issuers and sectors.
- Staying informed about economic conditions, interest rate movements, and credit developments.

CONCLUSION: BONDS OFFER INVESTORS A STEADY INCOME STREAM AND RELATIVE STABILITY, MAKING THEM AN ATTRACTIVE INVESTMENT OPTION. BY UNDERSTANDING THE BASICS OF BONDS, THE DIFFERENT TYPES AVAILABLE, AND THE ASSOCIATED RISKS, YOU CAN MAKE INFORMED DECISIONS WHEN INVESTING IN BONDS. REMEMBER TO CONSIDER YOUR INVESTMENT OBJECTIVES, RISK TOLERANCE, AND TIME HORIZON WHEN BUILDING A BOND PORTFOLIO. REGULAR MONITORING AND ADJUSTING OF YOUR BOND HOLDINGS WILL HELP ENSURE YOUR PORTFOLIO REMAINS ALIGNED WITH YOUR FINANCIAL GOALS.

Mutual Funds and Exchange-Traded Funds (ETFs)

MUTUAL FUNDS AND EXCHANGE-TRADED FUNDS (ETFS) ARE POPULAR INVESTMENT VEHICLES THAT PROVIDE INVESTORS WITH A CONVENIENT AND DIVERSIFIED WAY TO ACCESS A WIDE RANGE OF ASSET CLASSES. IN THIS CHAPTER, WE WILL EXPLORE THE BASICS OF MUTUAL FUNDS AND ETFS, THEIR BENEFITS, CONSIDERATIONS FOR INVESTING IN THEM, AND KEY DIFFERENCES BETWEEN THE TWO.

1. What are Mutual Funds?
   - Definition of mutual funds as investment vehicles that pool money from multiple investors to invest in a diversified portfolio of stocks, bonds, or other assets.
   - Explanation of how mutual funds are managed by professional fund managers.

2. What are ETFs?
   - Definition of ETFs as investment funds that trade on stock exchanges, similar to individual stocks.
   - Highlighting the key difference: ETFs can be bought and sold throughout the trading day, while mutual funds are priced once a day.

3. Benefits of Investing in Mutual Funds and ETFs:
   - Diversification: Mutual funds and ETFs provide access to a diversified portfolio of securities, reducing the risk associated with investing in individual stocks or bonds.
   - Professional Management: Funds are managed by experienced professionals who make investment decisions on behalf of the investors.

- Accessibility: Mutual funds and ETFs offer investors an opportunity to invest in various asset classes with relatively low investment amounts.
- Liquidity: ETFs can be bought and sold throughout the trading day at market prices, providing flexibility to investors.

4. Types of Mutual Funds:
- Equity Funds: Invest in stocks of companies to achieve capital appreciation.
- Bond Funds: Invest in bonds to generate income and potentially provide capital appreciation.
- Balanced Funds: Allocate investments between stocks and bonds to balance income and capital appreciation.
- Index Funds: Aim to replicate the performance of a specific market index, such as the S&P 500.
- Sector Funds: Concentrate investments in specific industry sectors, such as technology or healthcare.

5. Types of ETFs:
- Equity ETFs: Track specific stock market indices or sectors, providing investors exposure to a broad market or specific industry.
- Bond ETFs: Invest in bonds to generate income and potentially provide capital appreciation.
- Commodity ETFs: Track the performance of commodities like gold, oil, or agricultural products.
- Currency ETFs: Provide exposure to foreign currencies or currency baskets.

6. Key Differences between Mutual Funds and ETFs:
   - Trading: Mutual funds are bought and sold at the end-of-day net asset value (NAV), while ETFs trade on stock exchanges throughout the day at market prices.
   - Cost Structure: Mutual funds may charge sales loads and higher expense ratios, while ETFs generally have lower expense ratios.
   - Tax Efficiency: ETFs are typically more tax-efficient due to their unique structure, as they can minimize capital gains distributions.
   - Investment Minimums: Mutual funds may have minimum investment requirements, while ETFs can be bought with the price of a single share.

7. Considerations for Investing in Mutual Funds and ETFs:
   - Investment Objectives: Align the fund's investment strategy with your financial goals, risk tolerance, and time horizon.
   - Fees and Expenses: Compare expense ratios, sales loads, and transaction costs to select funds that align with your cost preferences.
   - Performance and Track Record: Evaluate a fund's historical performance, consistency, and long-term track record.
   - Fund Manager's Expertise: Research the experience and track record of the fund manager or management team.

8. Risks and Mitigation Strategies:
   - Market Risk: Mutual funds and ETFs are subject to market fluctuations and the inherent risks associated with the underlying assets.

- Manager Risk: Poor fund management decisions or changes in fund management can affect performance.
- Liquidity Risk: ETFs can be subject to liquidity risk if the underlying securities have limited trading activity.

9. Selecting the Right Mutual Funds and ETFs:
- Conduct thorough research and due diligence on the fund's investment strategy, historical performance, and risk profile.
- Consider asset allocation, diversification, and alignment with your investment objectives.
- Review prospectuses, annual reports, and other relevant fund documents before investing.

CONCLUSION: MUTUAL FUNDS AND ETFS OFFER INVESTORS ACCESS TO A DIVERSIFIED PORTFOLIO OF ASSETS, PROFESSIONAL MANAGEMENT, AND FLEXIBILITY. BY UNDERSTANDING THE BASICS OF THESE INVESTMENT VEHICLES, THEIR BENEFITS, CONSIDERATIONS, AND KEY DIFFERENCES, YOU CAN MAKE INFORMED DECISIONS WHEN BUILDING YOUR INVESTMENT PORTFOLIO. REMEMBER TO EVALUATE FUND PERFORMANCE, FEES, AND ALIGN YOUR INVESTMENTS WITH YOUR FINANCIAL GOALS AND RISK TOLERANCE. REGULAR MONITORING AND REVIEW OF YOUR MUTUAL FUND AND ETF HOLDINGS WILL HELP ENSURE YOUR PORTFOLIO REMAINS ALIGNED WITH YOUR INVESTMENT OBJECTIVES.

Diversification: The Key to Risk Management

DIVERSIFICATION IS A FUNDAMENTAL PRINCIPLE IN INVESTMENT MANAGEMENT THAT INVOLVES SPREADING INVESTMENTS ACROSS DIFFERENT ASSETS TO REDUCE RISK. IN THIS CHAPTER, WE WILL EXPLORE THE CONCEPT OF DIVERSIFICATION, ITS BENEFITS, AND STRATEGIES FOR IMPLEMENTING IT EFFECTIVELY.

1. Understanding Diversification:
   - Definition of diversification as the practice of spreading investments across different assets, such as stocks, bonds, real estate, and commodities.
   - Explanation of how diversification aims to reduce the impact of any single investment's performance on the overall portfolio.

2. Benefits of Diversification:
   - Risk Reduction: Diversification helps reduce the overall risk of a portfolio by avoiding overexposure to any single investment.
   - Smoother Returns: Diversified portfolios tend to experience less volatility and smoother returns over time.
   - Preservation of Capital: Diversification helps protect against significant losses by mitigating the impact of poor performance from individual investments.

3. Asset Allocation:
   - Definition of asset allocation as the process of determining the ideal mix of different asset classes in a portfolio.

- Importance of considering investment goals, risk tolerance, and time horizon when determining asset allocation.
- Common asset classes to consider: stocks, bonds, cash equivalents, real estate, and alternative investments.

4. Correlation and Covariance:
- Explanation of correlation as the statistical measure of how two investments move in relation to each other.
- Understanding covariance as a measure of the joint variability between two investments.
- Importance of selecting assets with low or negative correlation to achieve effective diversification.

5. Building a Diversified Portfolio:
- Spreading Investments Across Asset Classes: Allocating investments across different asset classes to reduce exposure to any single market or industry.
- Diversifying Within Asset Classes: Investing in a variety of securities within each asset class, such as stocks from different sectors or bonds with different maturities and credit ratings.
- Considering Global Diversification: Investing in assets across different countries and regions to mitigate country-specific risks.

6. Rebalancing:
- Definition of rebalancing as the process of realigning the portfolio back to the target asset allocation.
- Importance of regular portfolio reviews to rebalance and maintain the desired asset mix.
- Determining rebalancing triggers based on predetermined thresholds or time intervals.

7. **Diversification and Risk Management:**
   - **Mitigating Company-Specific Risk:** Diversification helps reduce the risk associated with investing in individual companies by spreading investments across multiple stocks.
   - **Managing Sector and Industry Risk:** Diversifying across different sectors and industries helps mitigate the impact of adverse events on a specific sector.
   - **Addressing Market and Systematic Risk:** Diversification helps manage broad market risks by including assets that have a low correlation with the overall market.

8. **Considerations for Effective Diversification:**
   - **Risk Tolerance and Investment Goals:** Consider your risk tolerance and investment objectives when determining the appropriate level of diversification.
   - **Adequate Portfolio Size:** Smaller portfolios may face limitations in achieving optimal diversification, so consider the impact of portfolio size on diversification effectiveness.
   - **Regular Monitoring and Adjustments:** Regularly review and adjust your portfolio to ensure it remains aligned with your diversification strategy.

9. **Limitations of Diversification:**
   - **Systematic Risks:** Diversification may not fully protect against broad market downturns or systemic risks that affect all investments.
   - **Over-Diversification:** Excessive diversification can lead to an overly diluted portfolio, reducing the potential for significant returns.

<u>**CONCLUSION:**</u> DIVERSIFICATION IS A CRUCIAL STRATEGY FOR RISK MANAGEMENT AND ACHIEVING LONG-TERM INVESTMENT SUCCESS. BY SPREADING INVESTMENTS ACROSS DIFFERENT ASSET CLASSES, SECTORS, AND REGIONS, INVESTORS CAN REDUCE RISK AND POTENTIALLY ENHANCE RETURNS. HOWEVER, DIVERSIFICATION DOES NOT GUARANTEE AGAINST LOSSES, AND CAREFUL CONSIDERATION OF INVESTMENT

Long-Term Investing and the Power of Compound Interest

LONG-TERM INVESTING IS A STRATEGY THAT EMPHASIZES HOLDING INVESTMENTS FOR AN EXTENDED PERIOD TO BENEFIT FROM THE POWER OF COMPOUND INTEREST. IN THIS FINAL CHAPTER, WE WILL EXPLORE THE CONCEPT OF LONG-TERM INVESTING, THE ROLE OF COMPOUND INTEREST IN WEALTH ACCUMULATION, AND KEY CONSIDERATIONS FOR IMPLEMENTING A SUCCESSFUL LONG-TERM INVESTMENT STRATEGY.

1. Understanding Long-Term Investing:
- Definition of long-term investing as a strategy that focuses on holding investments for an extended period, typically years or decades.
- Explanation of how long-term investing allows investors to benefit from the compounding of returns over time.

2. The Power of Compound Interest:
- Definition of compound interest as the concept of earning interest on both the initial investment and any accumulated interest over time.
- Illustration of how compound interest accelerates wealth accumulation and can significantly impact investment returns over long periods.

3. Time Horizon and Investment Goals:
- Importance of aligning investment decisions with your specific time horizon and financial goals.
- Exploring different investment goals such as retirement planning, education funding, or wealth accumulation.

4. Investing in Growth Assets:
   - Introduction to growth assets, such as stocks and equity funds, which have the potential for long-term capital appreciation.
   - Explanation of the historical performance of the stock market and its potential for delivering higher returns over the long run.

5. Dollar-Cost Averaging:
   - Definition of dollar-cost averaging as an investment strategy where fixed amounts of money are regularly invested in a particular asset, regardless of its price.
   - Explanation of how dollar-cost averaging can reduce the impact of market volatility and potentially improve long-term returns.

6. Benefits of Long-Term Investing:
   - Compounding Returns: Long-term investing allows investors to benefit from the compounding effect of returns over time.
   - Ride Out Market Volatility: Investing for the long term reduces the need to react to short-term market fluctuations and increases the likelihood of capturing long-term market growth.
   - Time for Recovery: Long-term investors have the advantage of giving their investments time to recover from market downturns.

7. Risk Management and Asset Allocation:
   - Importance of asset allocation in long-term investing to balance risk and return.

- Diversifying investments across different asset classes and sectors to manage risk and potentially enhance returns.
- Regularly reviewing and rebalancing the portfolio to maintain the desired asset allocation.

8. Emotional Discipline and Patience:
- Emphasizing the importance of emotional discipline in long-term investing to avoid making impulsive investment decisions based on short-term market fluctuations.
- Developing patience and staying committed to the long-term investment strategy, even during periods of market volatility.

9. Monitoring and Adjustments:
- Regularly monitoring the performance of the investment portfolio and staying informed about market trends and economic developments.
- Making strategic adjustments to the portfolio as needed based on changes in investment goals, risk tolerance, or market conditions.

10. Seeking Professional Advice:
- Considering the benefits of consulting with a financial advisor or investment professional to develop a long-term investment plan tailored to your specific needs and goals.

CONCLUSION: LONG-TERM INVESTING, COUPLED WITH THE POWER OF COMPOUND INTEREST, CAN SIGNIFICANTLY IMPACT WEALTH ACCUMULATION AND HELP INDIVIDUALS ACHIEVE THEIR FINANCIAL GOALS. BY ADOPTING A DISCIPLINED APPROACH, FOCUSING ON LONG-TERM GROWTH ASSETS, DIVERSIFYING INVESTMENTS, AND STAYING COMMITTED TO THE INVESTMENT STRATEGY, INVESTORS CAN ENHANCE THEIR CHANCES OF SUCCESS. REMEMBER, SUCCESSFUL LONG-TERM INVESTING REQUIRES PATIENCE, DISCIPLINE, AND A FOCUS ON THE BIGGER PICTURE RATHER THAN SHORT-TERM MARKET FLUCTUATIONS.

Investing in Real Estate

INVESTING IN REAL ESTATE CAN BE A LUCRATIVE AND REWARDING VENTURE. IT OFFERS THE POTENTIAL FOR LONG-TERM CAPITAL APPRECIATION, CASH FLOW, AND DIVERSIFICATION IN AN INVESTMENT PORTFOLIO. IN THIS CHAPTER, WE WILL EXPLORE THE BASICS OF INVESTING IN REAL ESTATE, DIFFERENT INVESTMENT OPTIONS, STRATEGIES, AND KEY CONSIDERATIONS FOR SUCCESS.

1. Understanding Real Estate Investments:
- Definition of real estate investments as the acquisition, ownership, and management of properties for the purpose of generating income or achieving capital appreciation.
- Highlighting the different types of real estate investments, including residential, commercial, industrial, and land.

2. Benefits of Real Estate Investing:
- Potential for Appreciation: Real estate has historically shown the potential for long-term value appreciation.
- Rental Income: Rental properties can generate a steady stream of income through monthly rent payments.
- Diversification: Real estate investments can provide diversification and serve as a hedge against other investment classes.
- Tangible Asset: Real estate investments offer the advantage of owning a physical asset with intrinsic value.

3. Investment Options in Real Estate:
- Residential Properties: Investing in single-family homes, condominiums, townhouses, or multi-family properties for rental income or resale.

- **Commercial Properties:** Investing in office buildings, retail spaces, industrial properties, or warehouses for lease to businesses.
- **Real Estate Investment Trusts (REITs):** Investing in publicly traded companies that own and manage income-generating real estate properties.
- **Real Estate Crowdfunding:** Participating in real estate projects by pooling funds with other investors through online platforms.

4. **Financing Real Estate Investments:**
   - **Obtaining Mortgage Loans:** Exploring traditional mortgage financing options to purchase properties.
   - **Alternative Financing:** Considering options such as seller financing, private loans, or partnerships to finance real estate investments.
   - **Evaluating Financing Costs:** Assessing interest rates, loan terms, and associated costs to determine the feasibility of financing options.

5. **Property Analysis and Due Diligence:**
   - **Conducting Market Research:** Analysing local real estate market conditions, supply and demand dynamics, and economic factors.
   - **Property Evaluation:** Assessing the physical condition, location, rental potential, and potential expenses associated with a property.
   - **Financial Analysis:** Evaluating the income potential, cash flow projections, and return on investment (ROI) for a property.

6. Risk Management and Property Management:
- Risk Assessment: Identifying and managing risks associated with real estate investments, such as vacancy rates, property damage, or changes in market conditions.
- Property Management: Considering the responsibilities of property management, such as tenant screening, lease agreements, property maintenance, and rent collection.
- Outsourcing Property Management: Evaluating the option of hiring a professional property management company to handle day-to-day operations.

7. Tax Considerations:
- Understanding Tax Benefits: Exploring tax advantages associated with real estate investments, such as depreciation deductions, mortgage interest deductions, and 1031 exchanges.
- Consulting with Tax Professionals: Seeking advice from tax professionals or accountants to optimize tax strategies and comply with applicable tax laws.

8. Exit Strategies:
- Sale for Profit: Selling a property for a profit when its value has appreciated significantly.
- Rental Income: Generating income from rental properties over the long term.
- 1031 Exchange: Utilizing a 1031 exchange to defer capital gains taxes by reinvesting proceeds into another qualified property.

9. Real Estate Investment Risks:
- Market Fluctuations: Real estate values can be affected by economic downturns, changes in interest rates, or local market conditions.

- **Property-Specific Risks:** Properties may experience vacancy, repairs, or unexpected expenses that can impact profitability.
- **Regulatory and Legal Risks:** Real estate investments are subject to zoning regulations, tenant rights, and legal disputes.

10. Building a Real Estate Portfolio:
- **Setting Investment Goals:** Defining investment objectives, risk tolerance, and time horizon for real estate investments.
- **Diversification:** Spreading investments across different property types, locations, or investment strategies.
- **Continual Learning:** Staying updated on market trends, investment strategies, and industry developments through research, education, and networking.

CONCLUSION: INVESTING IN REAL ESTATE OFFERS UNIQUE OPPORTUNITIES FOR WEALTH CREATION, INCOME GENERATION, AND PORTFOLIO DIVERSIFICATION. BY UNDERSTANDING THE FUNDAMENTALS OF REAL ESTATE INVESTMENTS, CONDUCTING THOROUGH DUE DILIGENCE, MANAGING RISKS EFFECTIVELY, AND STAYING INFORMED ABOUT MARKET TRENDS, INVESTORS CAN POSITION THEMSELVES FOR SUCCESS IN THE DYNAMIC WORLD OF REAL ESTATE INVESTING.

Building a Portfolio: Asset Allocation Strategies

BUILDING A WELL-STRUCTURED INVESTMENT PORTFOLIO IS ESSENTIAL FOR LONG-TERM FINANCIAL SUCCESS. ASSET ALLOCATION IS THE PROCESS OF DETERMINING HOW TO DISTRIBUTE INVESTMENTS ACROSS DIFFERENT ASSET CLASSES TO ACHIEVE SPECIFIC INVESTMENT GOALS WHILE MANAGING RISK. IN THIS CHAPTER, WE WILL EXPLORE VARIOUS ASSET ALLOCATION STRATEGIES AND CONSIDERATIONS FOR BUILDING A DIVERSIFIED PORTFOLIO.

1. Understanding Asset Allocation:
- Definition of asset allocation as the distribution of investments across different asset classes, such as stocks, bonds, cash, and alternative investments.
- Importance of asset allocation in managing risk, optimizing returns, and achieving investment objectives.

2. Investment Goals and Risk Tolerance:
- Setting Investment Goals: Defining your investment objectives, whether it's long-term growth, income generation, capital preservation, or a combination of these.
- Assessing Risk Tolerance: Evaluating your willingness and ability to take on risk, considering factors such as financial situation, time horizon, and personal comfort level.

3. Modern Portfolio Theory:
- Overview of Modern Portfolio Theory (MPT): The concept that a well-diversified portfolio can optimize returns for a given level of risk.

- Efficient Frontier: Understanding the concept of the efficient frontier, which represents the set of portfolios that offer the maximum expected return for a given level of risk.

4. Strategic Asset Allocation:
   - Strategic Asset Allocation: A long-term approach to asset allocation based on your investment goals and risk tolerance.
   - Establishing Target Allocations: Determining the desired allocation percentages for each asset class based on historical performance, expected returns, and risk characteristics.
   - Rebalancing: Periodically reviewing and adjusting the portfolio to maintain the desired asset allocation.

5. Tactical Asset Allocation:
   - Tactical Asset Allocation: A dynamic approach that involves actively adjusting the portfolio's asset allocation based on short-term market conditions and economic outlook.
   - Market Timing: Considerations and challenges associated with market timing and its potential impact on investment performance.

6. Core and Satellite Approach:
   - Core Holdings: Allocating a significant portion of the portfolio to a diversified set of low-cost, passive investments, such as index funds or ETFs, that represent the broader market.
   - Satellite Holdings: Adding smaller, more specialized investments, such as individual stocks, sector funds, or alternative investments, to potentially enhance returns or provide additional diversification.

7. Risk Parity Approach:
- Risk Parity: An asset allocation strategy that aims to allocate investments based on risk contributions rather than traditional market capitalization weights.
- Balancing Risk Factors: Considering factors such as volatility, correlation, and risk exposure to achieve a more balanced risk profile across the portfolio.

8. Considerations for Diversification:
- Geographic Diversification: Spreading investments across different countries and regions to mitigate country-specific risks.
- Sector Diversification: Allocating investments across various sectors and industries to reduce exposure to specific market or industry risks.
- Asset Class Diversification: Balancing investments across different asset classes, such as stocks, bonds, cash, and alternative investments.

9. Reviewing and Rebalancing:
- Regular Portfolio Reviews: Conducting periodic reviews to assess the performance, risk profile, and alignment with investment goals.
- Rebalancing Strategies: Determining the frequency and triggers for rebalancing the portfolio, such as specific asset class deviations or predetermined time intervals.

10. Seeking Professional Advice:
- Consulting with a Financial Advisor: Considering the benefits of seeking advice from a qualified financial advisor to develop and implement an asset allocation strategy tailored to your specific needs and goals.

CONCLUSION: BUILDING A WELL-DIVERSIFIED INVESTMENT PORTFOLIO REQUIRES CAREFUL CONSIDERATION OF ASSET ALLOCATION STRATEGIES, INVESTMENT GOALS, AND RISK TOLERANCE. BY APPLYING APPROPRIATE ASSET ALLOCATION TECHNIQUES, MAINTAINING A BALANCED PORTFOLIO, AND PERIODICALLY REVIEWING AND REBALANCING INVESTMENTS, INVESTORS CAN POSITION THEMSELVES FOR LONG-TERM SUCCESS. REMEMBER, ASSET ALLOCATION

The Importance of Research and Due Diligence

RESEARCH AND DUE DILIGENCE ARE CRITICAL ASPECTS OF SUCCESSFUL INVESTING. THEY PROVIDE INVESTORS WITH THE NECESSARY KNOWLEDGE AND INFORMATION TO MAKE INFORMED DECISIONS, MANAGE RISKS, AND MAXIMIZE POTENTIAL RETURNS. IN THIS CHAPTER, WE WILL EXPLORE THE IMPORTANCE OF RESEARCH AND DUE DILIGENCE IN THE INVESTMENT PROCESS AND PROVIDE GUIDANCE ON CONDUCTING THOROUGH ANALYSIS.

1. The Role of Research in Investing:
- Understanding Research: Research involves gathering, analyzing, and interpreting information to gain insights into investment opportunities, market trends, and economic conditions.
- Making Informed Decisions: Research empowers investors to make informed decisions based on thorough analysis and understanding of the investment landscape.

2. Fundamental Analysis:
- Fundamental Analysis: The process of evaluating the financial health, performance, and prospects of an individual company or investment.
- Financial Statements: Analyzing company financial statements, including balance sheets, income statements, and cash flow statements, to assess financial strength and profitability.
- Business Model and Competitive Advantage: Evaluating a company's business model, competitive position, and unique advantages to determine its potential for long-term success.

3. Technical Analysis:
   - Technical Analysis: The study of historical price and volume data to identify patterns, trends, and potential market movements.
   - Charts and Indicators: Using charts, trend lines, moving averages, and other technical indicators to analyze price patterns and make predictions about future price movements.
   - Limitations of Technical Analysis: Recognizing that technical analysis alone may not provide a complete picture and should be used in conjunction with other forms of analysis.

4. Economic Analysis:
   - Economic Indicators: Monitoring key economic indicators, such as GDP growth, inflation rates, interest rates, and employment data, to understand the overall health of the economy.
   - Industry and Sector Analysis: Assessing the performance, trends, and outlook of specific industries or sectors to identify investment opportunities and potential risks.

5. Risk Assessment:
   - Risk Identification: Identifying and evaluating various types of investment risks, including market risk, credit risk, liquidity risk, and geopolitical risk.
   - Risk-Return Tradeoff: Understanding the relationship between risk and potential returns and assessing whether the potential rewards justify the level of risk.
   - Stress Testing: Conducting scenario analysis and stress tests to assess how investments may perform under adverse market conditions.

6. Due Diligence:
   - Conducting Due Diligence: The process of thoroughly researching and investigating an investment opportunity or asset before making a commitment.
   - Company or Asset Analysis: Examining relevant information about a company, such as its financials, management team, competitive landscape, and growth prospects.
   - Legal and Regulatory Compliance: Verifying that the investment opportunity complies with applicable laws, regulations, and industry standards.
   - Evaluating Investment Partners: Assessing the track record, reputation, and credibility of investment partners or managers before entrusting them with funds.

7. Information Sources:
   - Utilizing Multiple Sources: Gathering information from various sources, including financial publications, company reports, industry research, and reputable websites.
   - Expert Opinions: Considering the insights and analysis provided by experts, financial analysts, and reputable investment firms.
   - Data Analytics and Technology: Leveraging data analytics tools and technology platforms to access and analyze vast amounts of data efficiently.

8. Continuous Learning:
   - Staying Informed: Recognizing that the investment landscape is dynamic and constantly evolving, and staying updated on market trends, new investment opportunities, and regulatory changes.

- Investment Education: Continuously expanding knowledge and skills through investment courses, workshops, books, and online resources.
- Learning from Mistakes: Embracing mistakes as learning opportunities and using them to refine investment strategies and decision-making processes.

9. Emotional Discipline:
- Emotion vs. Rationality: Recognizing the influence of emotions, such as fear and greed, on investment decisions and practicing disciplined, rational decision-making.
- Long-Term Perspective: Focusing on long-term investment objectives and avoiding impulsive reactions to short-term market fluctuations.

<u>CONCLUSION:</u> RESEARCH AND DUE DILIGENCE ARE CRUCIAL COMPONENTS OF SUCCESSFUL INVESTING. BY CONDUCTING THOROUGH ANALYSIS, STAYING INFORMED, AND MAKING INFORMED DECISIONS BASED ON SOUND RESEARCH, INVESTORS CAN ENHANCE THEIR UNDERSTANDING OF INVESTMENT OPPORTUNITIES, MANAGE RISKS EFFECTIVELY, AND IMPROVE THEIR CHANCES OF ACHIEVING THEIR FINANCIAL GOALS. REMEMBER, DILIGENCE AND CONTINUOUS LEARNING ARE KEY TO SUCCESS IN THE DYNAMIC WORLD OF INVESTING.

Tax Considerations and Retirement Accounts

UNDERSTANDING TAX CONSIDERATIONS AND UTILIZING RETIREMENT ACCOUNTS EFFECTIVELY CAN SIGNIFICANTLY IMPACT YOUR INVESTMENT RETURNS AND LONG-TERM FINANCIAL GOALS. THIS CHAPTER EXPLORES THE IMPORTANCE OF TAX PLANNING, TAX-EFFICIENT INVESTING, AND THE BENEFITS OF RETIREMENT ACCOUNTS FOR MAXIMIZING SAVINGS AND MINIMIZING TAX LIABILITIES.

1. The Role of Taxes in Investing:
- Tax Efficiency: Recognizing that taxes can erode investment returns and the importance of tax-efficient strategies to minimize tax liabilities.
- Types of Taxes: Understanding different types of taxes, including capital gains tax, income tax, dividends tax, and estate tax.

2. Tax Planning Strategies:
- Asset Location: Placing investments in tax-advantaged accounts, such as retirement accounts, to defer or minimize taxes.
- Tax-Loss Harvesting: Offsetting capital gains with capital losses to reduce taxable income.
- Holding Periods: Taking advantage of long-term capital gains tax rates by holding investments for more than one year.
- Qualified Dividends: Considering investments that generate qualified dividends, which are taxed at lower rates.
- Tax-Efficient Fund Selection: Choosing investment funds with low turnover and tax-efficient strategies to minimize taxable distributions.

3. Retirement Accounts:
   - Individual Retirement Accounts (IRAs): Exploring the benefits of Traditional IRAs and Roth IRAs, including tax-deferred growth or tax-free withdrawals in retirement.
   - 401(k) Plans: Understanding employer-sponsored retirement plans, their contribution limits, and potential employer matching contributions.
   - SEP IRAs and SIMPLE IRAs: Exploring retirement account options for self-employed individuals or small business owners.
   - Health Savings Accounts (HSAs): Recognizing the tax advantages of HSAs for individuals with high-deductible health insurance plans, including tax-deductible contributions and tax-free withdrawals for qualified medical expenses.

4. Contributions and Contribution Limits:
   - Understanding contribution limits for different retirement accounts, including annual contribution limits and catch-up contributions for individuals aged 50 and older.
   - Maximizing Contributions: Taking advantage of the maximum allowable contributions to retirement accounts to optimize long-term savings and tax benefits.

5. Required Minimum Distributions (RMDs):
   - RMD Basics: Understanding the requirement to start taking minimum distributions from retirement accounts after reaching a certain age (currently 72 for most retirement accounts).

- Calculating RMDs: Familiarizing yourself with the IRS guidelines for calculating RMD amounts based on your account balances and life expectancy.
- Penalty for Noncompliance: Recognizing the significant penalties for failing to take RMDs as required.

6. Roth Conversions and Backdoor Roth IRAs:
- Roth Conversions: Considering the option to convert Traditional IRA funds into a Roth IRA to potentially enjoy tax-free withdrawals in retirement.
- Backdoor Roth IRAs: Exploring the strategy of making non-deductible contributions to a Traditional IRA and then converting it to a Roth IRA, bypassing income limits for direct Roth IRA contributions.

7. Estate Planning and Inheritance:
- Estate Tax Considerations: Understanding the potential impact of estate taxes on your assets and exploring estate planning strategies to minimize tax liabilities.
- Beneficiary Designations: Reviewing and updating beneficiary designations for retirement accounts to ensure a smooth transfer of assets and potential tax advantages.

8. Tax-Advantaged Investments:
- Municipal Bonds: Considering the tax benefits of investing in municipal bonds, which are often tax-free at the federal level and potentially tax-free at the state and local levels.
- 529 College Savings Plans: Exploring the tax advantages of 529 plans, including tax-deferred growth and tax-free withdrawals for qualified education expenses.

9. **Seeking Professional Tax Advice:**
   - **Consulting with a Tax Professional:** Recognizing the complexity of tax laws and the value of seeking advice from a qualified tax professional or accountant for personalized tax planning and strategies.

CONCLUSION: TAX CONSIDERATIONS AND RETIREMENT ACCOUNTS PLAY A CRUCIAL ROLE IN MAXIMIZING INVESTMENT RETURNS AND LONG-TERM FINANCIAL SUCCESS. BY IMPLEMENTING TAX-EFFICIENT STRATEGIES, TAKING ADVANTAGE OF RETIREMENT ACCOUNTS, AND STAYING INFORMED ABOUT TAX LAWS AND REGULATIONS, INVESTORS CAN MINIMIZE TAX LIABILITIES, OPTIMIZE SAVINGS, AND ACHIEVE THEIR RETIREMENT GOALS. REMEMBER, TAX PLANNING SHOULD BE AN INTEGRAL PART OF YOUR OVERALL INVESTMENT STRATEGY FOR LONG-TERM FINANCIAL WELL-BEING.

Developing an Investment Plan

DEVELOPING A COMPREHENSIVE INVESTMENT PLAN IS ESSENTIAL FOR ACHIEVING FINANCIAL GOALS, MANAGING RISKS, AND MAKING INFORMED INVESTMENT DECISIONS. IN THIS CHAPTER, WE WILL DISCUSS THE KEY STEPS INVOLVED IN CREATING AN INVESTMENT PLAN THAT ALIGNS WITH YOUR OBJECTIVES, RISK TOLERANCE, AND TIME HORIZON.

1. Assessing Your Financial Situation:
- Evaluating your current financial situation, including income, expenses, assets, and liabilities.
- Identifying your short-term and long-term financial goals, such as saving for retirement, purchasing a home, or funding education.

2. Defining Investment Objectives:
- Setting clear and specific investment objectives, considering factors such as growth, income, capital preservation, and time horizon.
- Prioritizing your investment goals based on importance and urgency.

3. Determining Risk Tolerance:
- Assessing your risk tolerance by considering your financial capacity to handle risk and your emotional comfort level.
- Understanding the relationship between risk and potential returns and aligning your risk tolerance with your investment goals.

4. Asset Allocation:
- Allocating your investments across different asset classes, such as stocks, bonds, cash, and alternative investments.
-

- Determining the optimal asset allocation based on your investment goals, risk tolerance, and time horizon.
- Rebalancing the portfolio periodically to maintain the desired asset allocation.

5. Selecting Investments:
   - Conducting research and due diligence to identify suitable investments that align with your investment plan.
   - Considering factors such as investment performance, historical data, financial health, and management quality.
   - Diversifying your portfolio by selecting investments from various industries, sectors, and geographic locations.

6. Implementing the Investment Plan:
   - Opening investment accounts, such as brokerage accounts, retirement accounts, or education savings accounts, based on your specific needs.
   - Executing trades and purchasing investments in line with your asset allocation and investment objectives.

7. Monitoring and Reviewing:
   - Monitoring the performance of your investments regularly and comparing it against your investment plan and benchmarks.
   - Reviewing the progress towards your financial goals and making adjustments as needed.
   - Staying informed about market trends, economic developments, and changes in investment strategies.

8. Tax Planning and Optimization:
- Incorporating tax-efficient strategies, such as utilizing retirement accounts, tax-loss harvesting, and maximizing tax-advantaged investments.
- Consulting with a tax professional to optimize tax planning and minimize tax liabilities.

9. Regular Contributions and Dollar-Cost Averaging:
- Implementing a disciplined approach by making regular contributions to your investment accounts.
- Using dollar-cost averaging to invest a fixed amount of money at regular intervals, reducing the impact of market volatility.

10. Seeking Professional Advice:
- Considering the benefits of consulting with a qualified financial advisor or investment professional to provide guidance and expertise.
- Utilizing their knowledge and experience to align your investment plan with your financial goals and risk tolerance.

CONCLUSION: DEVELOPING AN INVESTMENT PLAN IS A CRITICAL STEP TOWARDS ACHIEVING YOUR FINANCIAL GOALS AND BUILDING LONG-TERM WEALTH. BY ASSESSING YOUR FINANCIAL SITUATION, DEFINING OBJECTIVES, DETERMINING RISK TOLERANCE, AND IMPLEMENTING A WELL-ROUNDED INVESTMENT STRATEGY, YOU CAN NAVIGATE THE INVESTMENT LANDSCAPE WITH CONFIDENCE AND INCREASE YOUR CHANCES OF FINANCIAL SUCCESS. REMEMBER, AN INVESTMENT PLAN IS A DYNAMIC DOCUMENT THAT REQUIRES PERIODIC REVIEW AND ADJUSTMENT AS YOUR CIRCUMSTANCES AND MARKET CONDITIONS CHANGE.

Staying Informed and Adapting to Market Changes

STAYING INFORMED ABOUT MARKET TRENDS, ECONOMIC DEVELOPMENTS, AND ADAPTING TO MARKET CHANGES IS CRUCIAL FOR SUCCESSFUL INVESTING. IN THIS CHAPTER, WE WILL EXPLORE THE IMPORTANCE OF STAYING INFORMED, UTILIZING VARIOUS INFORMATION SOURCES, AND MAKING INFORMED DECISIONS IN RESPONSE TO EVOLVING MARKET CONDITIONS.

1. Continuous Learning:
   - Embracing a learning mindset and recognizing that the investment landscape is dynamic and constantly evolving.
   - Engaging in continuous learning through reading books, articles, attending seminars, webinars, and participating in investment forums or communities.

2. Market Research:
   - Utilizing reliable and reputable sources for market research, such as financial publications, news outlets, research reports, and government publications.
   - Monitoring economic indicators, industry trends, and company-specific news to gain insights into market conditions and investment opportunities.

3. Fundamental Analysis:
   - Conducting thorough fundamental analysis to assess the financial health, performance, and prospects of individual companies or investments.
   - Analysing financial statements, industry trends, competitive landscapes, and growth prospects to make informed investment decisions.

4. Technical Analysis:
   - Incorporating technical analysis as a tool to study historical price and volume data, identify patterns, and make predictions about future market movements.
   - Using charts, indicators, and trend lines to gain insights into market trends, support, and resistance levels.

5. News and Market Sentiment:
   - Staying informed about news and market sentiment that can influence market movements and investor behavior.
   - Evaluating the impact of news events, geopolitical developments, and economic indicators on specific investments and overall market sentiment.

6. Investment Newsletters and Research Reports:
   - Subscribing to reputable investment newsletters and research reports that provide insights, analysis, and recommendations on various investment opportunities.
   - Reviewing the track record and credibility of the sources before relying on their recommendations.

7. Financial Advisor and Investment Professionals:
   - Engaging with qualified financial advisors or investment professionals who can provide expert advice and guidance based on their knowledge and experience.
   - Regularly communicating with your financial advisor to discuss investment strategies, review performance, and adapt to changing market conditions.

8. **Market Volatility and Risk Management:**
   - Recognizing that markets can be volatile and subject to rapid changes.
   - Implementing risk management strategies, such as diversification, asset allocation, and stop-loss orders, to mitigate the impact of market volatility.

9. **Adapting to Changing Market Conditions:**
   - Being flexible and adaptable to adjust investment strategies based on changing market conditions.
   - Recognizing the need to rebalance portfolios, adjust asset allocation, and reallocate investments to align with evolving market trends and economic outlooks.

10. **Emotion Management:**
    - Keeping emotions in check and making rational investment decisions based on thorough analysis and research.
    - Avoiding impulsive reactions to short-term market fluctuations and maintaining a long-term perspective.

CONCLUSION: STAYING INFORMED AND ADAPTING TO MARKET CHANGES ARE ESSENTIAL FOR SUCCESSFUL INVESTING. BY CONTINUOUSLY LEARNING, CONDUCTING THOROUGH RESEARCH, AND UTILIZING RELIABLE INFORMATION SOURCES, INVESTORS CAN MAKE INFORMED DECISIONS, MANAGE RISKS, AND CAPITALIZE ON INVESTMENT OPPORTUNITIES. REMEMBER, MARKET CONDITIONS CAN CHANGE RAPIDLY, AND STAYING PROACTIVE AND FLEXIBLE IN YOUR INVESTMENT APPROACH IS CRUCIAL FOR LONG-TERM SUCCESS.

Common Pitfalls and How to Avoid Them

INVESTING COMES WITH ITS FAIR SHARE OF CHALLENGES AND POTENTIAL PITFALLS. IN THIS CHAPTER, WE WILL DISCUSS SOME COMMON PITFALLS THAT INVESTORS OFTEN ENCOUNTER AND PROVIDE STRATEGIES TO AVOID THEM. BY BEING AWARE OF THESE PITFALLS AND IMPLEMENTING PREVENTIVE MEASURES, YOU CAN NAVIGATE THE INVESTMENT LANDSCAPE MORE EFFECTIVELY AND INCREASE YOUR CHANCES OF SUCCESS.

1. Emotional Decision Making:
- Recognizing the impact of emotions, such as fear and greed, on investment decisions.
- Implementing strategies to manage emotions, such as maintaining a long-term perspective, sticking to your investment plan, and avoiding impulsive reactions to market fluctuations.

2. Lack of Research and Due Diligence:
- Conducting thorough research and due diligence before making investment decisions.
- Reviewing financial statements, analyzing company fundamentals, and understanding the risks and potential returns of investments.

3. Overconfidence and Overtrading:
- Avoiding overconfidence in your investment abilities and recognizing the limitations of your knowledge and expertise.
- Resisting the urge to engage in excessive trading, as it can lead to increased transaction costs and potential losses.

4. **Lack of Diversification:**
   - Recognizing the importance of diversification in managing risk.
   - Spreading investments across different asset classes, industries, and geographic locations to reduce the impact of individual investment failures.

5. **Chasing Hot Tips and Market Hype:**
   - Avoiding the temptation to chase hot tips or investment fads without conducting proper research and analysis.
   - Relying on reputable sources of information and making informed decisions based on thorough evaluation.

6. **Market Timing:**
   - Acknowledging the difficulty of consistently timing the market.
   - Adhering to a disciplined investment approach and focusing on long-term goals rather than attempting to predict short-term market movements.

7. **Neglecting to Rebalance:**
   - Regularly reviewing and rebalancing your investment portfolio to maintain the desired asset allocation.
   - Selling overperforming investments and buying underperforming ones to align with your investment plan.

8. **Failure to Set Realistic Expectations:**
   - Setting realistic expectations for investment returns based on historical performance and market conditions.
   - Understanding that investments carry inherent risks and that returns may vary over time.

9. **Neglecting Tax Considerations:**
   - Incorporating tax planning into your investment strategy to optimize tax efficiency.
   - Utilizing tax-advantaged accounts and considering the tax implications of investment decisions.

10. **Lack of Patience and Discipline:**
    - Exercising patience and discipline in your investment approach.
    - Avoiding impulsive decisions and staying committed to your long-term investment plan.

<u>CONCLUSION</u>: BY BEING AWARE OF THESE COMMON PITFALLS AND IMPLEMENTING STRATEGIES TO AVOID THEM, YOU CAN ENHANCE YOUR INVESTMENT JOURNEY AND IMPROVE YOUR CHANCES OF SUCCESS. REMEMBER, INVESTING IS A LONG-TERM ENDEAVOR THAT REQUIRES DISCIPLINE, RESEARCH, AND INFORMED DECISION-MAKING. BY STAYING FOCUSED, MANAGING EMOTIONS, CONDUCTING THOROUGH RESEARCH, AND MAINTAINING A DISCIPLINED APPROACH, YOU CAN NAVIGATE THE INVESTMENT LANDSCAPE MORE EFFECTIVELY AND ACHIEVE YOUR FINANCIAL GOALS.

Conclusion: Your Journey Begins Here

Congratulations! You have reached the end of this book on how to invest your money for beginners. Throughout this journey, we have covered a wide range of topics, from setting financial goals to understanding different investment options, creating a budget, and developing an investment plan. We have explored the importance of risk management, the power of compound interest, and the significance of staying informed and adapting to market changes. We have also highlighted common pitfalls and provided strategies to avoid them.

Remember, investing is a lifelong learning process. It requires continuous education, research, and adaptation to changing market conditions. The knowledge and insights you have gained from this book provide a strong foundation to embark on your investment journey.

As you move forward, keep in mind that investing involves risks, and there are no guarantees of success. However, by following the principles and strategies outlined in this book, you can position yourself for long-term financial growth and increase the likelihood of achieving your investment goals.

Always be mindful of your risk tolerance, financial objectives, and time horizon when making investment decisions. Regularly review and adjust your investment plan as needed, considering changes in your personal circumstances and market dynamics.

Additionally, seek professional advice when necessary, whether it's from a financial advisor, tax professional, or legal expert. Their guidance can provide valuable insights and help you make informed decisions aligned with your specific needs.

Finally, remember that investing is not solely about financial gains. It's also about creating a secure future, achieving your dreams, and attaining financial freedom. Stay focused, remain disciplined, and be patient during both prosperous and challenging times.

With the knowledge gained from this book and a commitment to continuous learning, you are well-equipped to navigate the world of investing. Embrace this exciting journey, make sound investment decisions, and work towards a prosperous financial future.

WISHING YOU SUCCESS AND FULFILMENT IN YOUR INVESTMENT ENDEAVOURS. YOUR JOURNEY BEGINS HERE!

www.ingramcontent.com/pod-product-compliance
Lightning Source LLC
Chambersburg PA
CBHW030036230526
45472CB00002B/531